About me

W0099555

School: _____

Class: _____

Write 'hello' in your language(s).

My language skills

Match the pictures.

I can ... Units 1-3

	Colour the face: I can do it!

1 🎧 Listen and point.

1 2 3 4 5
6 7 8 9 10

| 1 |  |

2 💬 Say the words.

| 2 |  |

3 🔍 Read and match.

3   **4**   **5**   **6**

| 3 |  |

4 ✏️ Write.

My name's _____ .

I'm _____ years old.

| 4 |  |

3

I can ...   **Units 4-6**

<table>
<tr><td></td><td>Colour the face: I can do it!</td></tr>
</table>

1  Listen and point.

| 1 | 😊 |

2  Say the words.

| 2 | 😊 |

3  Read and draw.

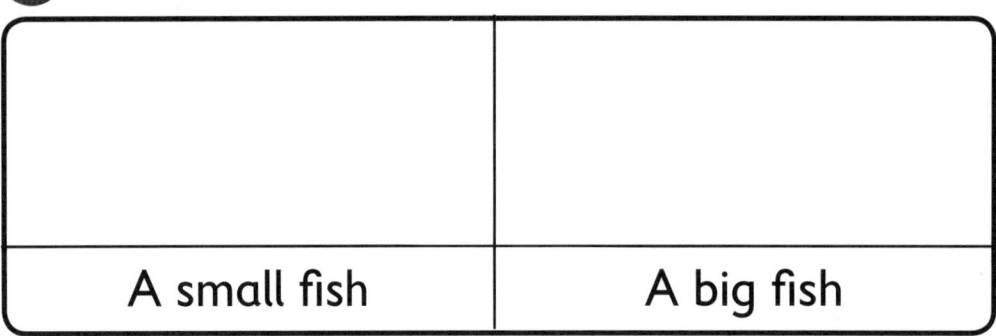

A small fish	A big fish

| 3 | 😊 |

4  Write the words.

eyes
ears
nose
mouth

| 4 | 😊 |

I can ...   Units 7-9

	Colour the face: I can do it!

1  Listen and point.

1	☺

2  Say the words.

2	☺

3 🔍 Read and colour.

She's got a yellow
T-shirt and a blue skirt.

He's got a green
T-shirt and red trousers.

3	☺

4 ✏️ Write what you can do.

I can _____ .

4	☺

I can ... Units 10-12

	Colour the face: I can do it!

1  Listen and point. What are they doing?

1

2 Say the words.

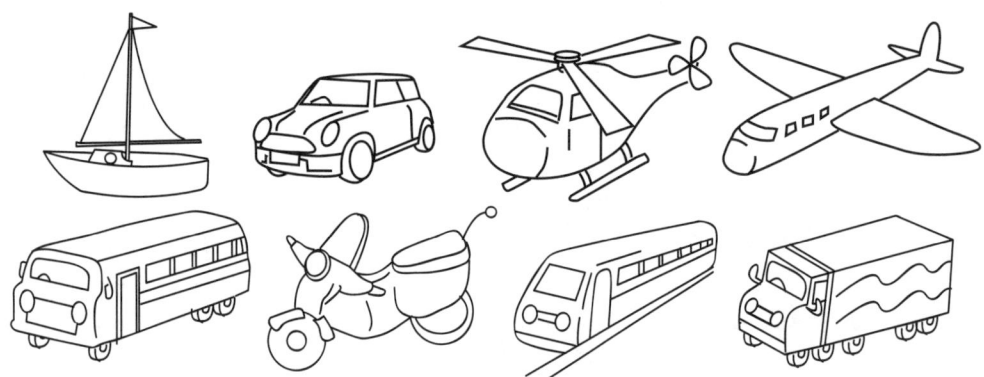

2

3 Read and draw.

She's eating an ice cream.   He's eating an apple.

3

4 Write three foods you like.

I like _____ , _____ and _____ .

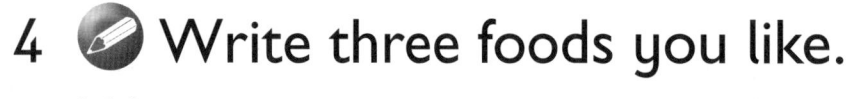

4

English and me

Colour the face. English is:

☺ OK   ☺ Good   ☺ Great   ☺ Fantastic

An English song I can sing:

- -

An English book I can read:

- -

English words I know:

Wow!

My classroom

Draw a picture of your classroom.

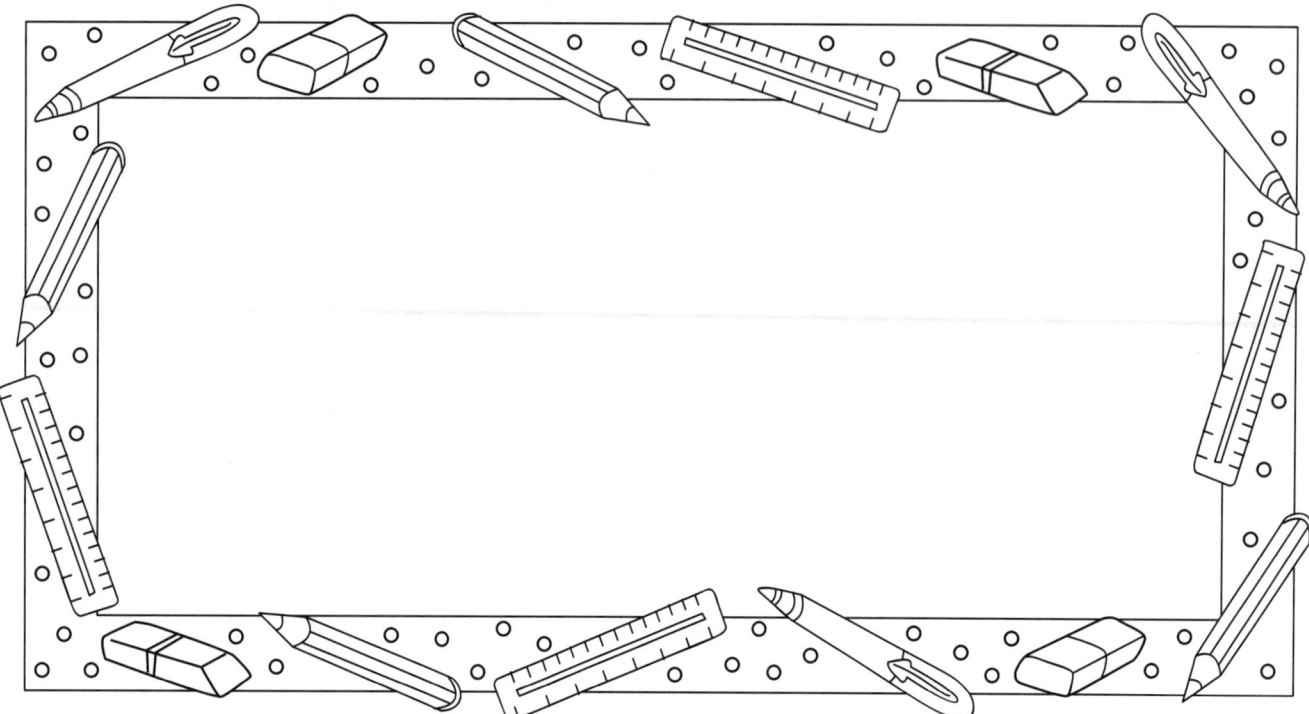

Now draw your school things.

My bag.

My table.

My pencil case.

My eraser.

About me

Draw or stick pictures of your favourite things.

My favourite number.

My favourite colour.

My favourite toy.

My favourite animal.

My pet

Draw a picture of your favourite pet.

Animal: --

Name: --

Colour: ---

10

Fun time

Draw a picture of something you like doing.

Answer the questions. Tick (✓) the boxes.
Can you ...

... play football?   Yes ☐ No ☐

... swim?   Yes ☐ No ☐

... play the guitar?   Yes ☐ No ☐

... ride a bike?   Yes ☐ No ☐

... play tennis?   Yes ☐ No ☐

My house

Draw a picture or stick a photo of your house.

Tick (✓) the boxes.

My house is   big ☐ small ☐

My house has got a kitchen ☐ a living room ☐ a hall ☐

a dining room ☐ a bathroom ☐ bedrooms ☐

How many bedrooms are there?   1 ☐ 2 ☐ 3 ☐

4 ☐ More! ☐

Food

Draw or stick pictures of food. Can you write the food words?

I like … ☺	I don't like … ☹

Second Edition

Kid's Box 1
Language Portfolio

This Language Portfolio allows your pupils to build a record of their progress through the school year.

The content follows the units of **Kid's Box** and the structure corresponds to that outlined by the Council of Europe's European Language Portfolio.

Please visit our website to download the Language Portfolio teaching notes.

www.cambridge.org/kidsbox

CAMBRIDGE
UNIVERSITY PRESS

ISBN 978-1-107-64976-7

9 781107 649767 >